SMARTS IS . . .

never letting a computer get you a date

advice from **Felix the Cat**

by Frank Hill

SMARTS IS...never letting a computer get you a date. Frank Hill.

Published by Determined Productions, Inc.
Box 2150, San Francisco, California 94126

ISBN 0-915696-61-4
LCCC No. 82-74028
First Printing

Printed in the United States of America

When it comes to giving advice, who could be better qualified than FELIX the Cat—the longevity champ of all time, who catapulted himself to fame first as an animated cartoon superstar of the 20's and 30's, then as an internationally loved comic strip character for decades through the 50's, to a TV star of the 60's.

Oh, yes, we know there are cats—and cats—some better known than others, but FELIX is not only the world's most famous, he's the funniest cat. You never know where he'll pop up next. Here he is starring again—this time in this little book of original cartoons which we hope will put you in the best of humor, perhaps make you laugh nine times as many times as a cat has lives.

Smarts is making reservations.

Smarts is feeling good about yourself.

Smarts is knowing what to pass up.

Smarts is being able to bounce back.

Smarts is checking the expiration date.

Smarts is keeping it simple.

Smarts is being able to break bad habits.

Smarts is insisting on fresh fish.

Smarts is motivating your employees.

Smarts is knowing how to juggle your budget.

Smarts is not drying your ski socks in the microwave.

Smarts is not coming on too strong.

Smarts is knowing when to ask for a raise.

Smarts is taking your banker to lunch.

Smarts is not getting in with the wrong crowd.

Smarts is keeping alert on the job.

Smarts is knowing which strings to pull.

Smarts is asking for a second opinion.

Smarts is doubling output without increasing overhead.

Smarts is surrounding yourself with loyal friends.

Smarts is knowing how to get your waiter's attention.

Smarts is not being jealous.

Smarts is knowing your market.

Smarts is having powerful friends.

Smarts is recognizing when "it's all over."

Smarts is knowing when to lose a contact lens.

Smarts is finding someone who worships you.

Smarts is knowing when to "lie low."

Smarts is realizing that you're not the only one with fantasies.

Smarts is being ready for anything.

Smarts is staying in control.

Smarts is keeping your act up to date.

Smarts is not jeopardizing your career.

Smarts is knowing when to bail out.

Smarts is not being distracted from the really important things.

Smarts is a sure-fire sales presentation.

Smarts is telling the truth.

Smarts is knowing how to stay on schedule.

Smarts is not being put off by first impressions.

Smarts is not running around with a short fuse.

Smarts is finding the right work-out program.

Smarts is keeping your feet on the ground.

Smarts is remembering to send your compliments to the chef.

Smarts is knowing how to get your dime back.

Smarts is watching where you step.

Smarts is making your own coffee.

Smarts is knowing that "estimates" are laughable.

Smarts is knowing when to look for a new job.

Smarts is not calling her by someone else's name.

Smarts is knowing when to put on the brakes.

Smarts is having a reliable source.

Smarts is doing as the Romans do.

Smarts is knowing that most people don't really want your advice.

Smarts is watching what you eat.

Smarts is never looking guilty.

Smarts is knowing whose space to stay out of.

Smarts is turning down that last cup of coffee.

Smarts is staying out of "clip joints."

Smarts is using all your assets.

Smarts is knowing when to retreat.

Smarts is drinking with the devil and not having to pay.

Smarts is knowing when to miss the boat.

Smarts is seeing your dentist regularly.

Smarts is owning your own airline.

Smarts is knowing whom to bring home to mother.

Smarts is bringing your own bottle.

Smarts is knowing when to stay down.

Smarts is staying loose.

Smarts is being able to make things go your way.

Smarts is knowing how to stay ahead.

Smarts is making good connections.

Smarts is carrying complete coverage.

Smarts is knowing how to make others feel comfortable.

Smarts is knowing how to score in a singles bar.

Smarts is staying out of bad neighborhoods.

Smarts is having the last laugh.